A–Z of Sharks

A–Z of Sharks

The alphabet of the shark world, from Angel Shark to Zebra Shark

Paula Hammond

amber
BOOKS

Published by
Amber Books Ltd
74–77 White Lion Street
London
N1 9PF
United Kingdom
www.amberbooks.co.uk
Appstore: itunes.com/apps/amberbooksltd
Facebook: www.facebook.com/amberbooks
Twitter: @amberbooks

ISBN: 978-1-78274-523-5

Project Editor: Sarah Uttridge
Design: Keren Harragan
Illustrator: JB Illustrations

Printed in Shenzhen, China

Contents

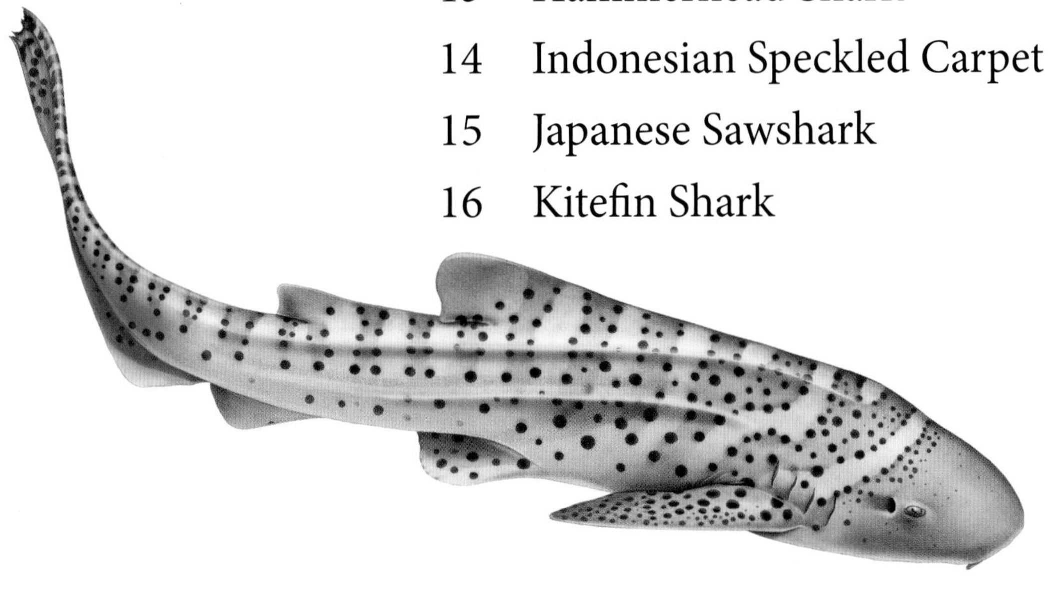

Aa

Angel Shark

Hides on sandy seafloors.

Fins

Fins help fish swim. This shark's fins look like angel wings.

It grows up to 6.5 feet (1.98 meters) long.

Mouth

This shark has several rows of teeth in its wide mouth.

Bull Shark

Bb

Hunts in warm waters.

Females grow bigger than males.

Body
Most sharks live in oceans. A bull shark can also live in rivers.

Attack
It's called a bull shark because it attacks head first, like a bull.

Cc Caribbean Reef Shark

Sometimes sleeps in sea caves.

Eyes
This shark can see better than other sharks as its eyes are bigger.

This shark has 4 to 6 pups (babies) at a time.

Body
It can turn its stomach inside out to remove anything nasty in there.

Dogfish Shark

Dd

World's most common shark.

Poison Spikes
In front of each dorsal (back) fin is a spike. It holds poison.

Groups
It's called a dogfish shark because it lives in groups, like dogs.

It eats fish, squid, and octopus.

Ee Epaulette Shark

Likes shallow pools and reefs.

This shark can walk on dry land when hunting.

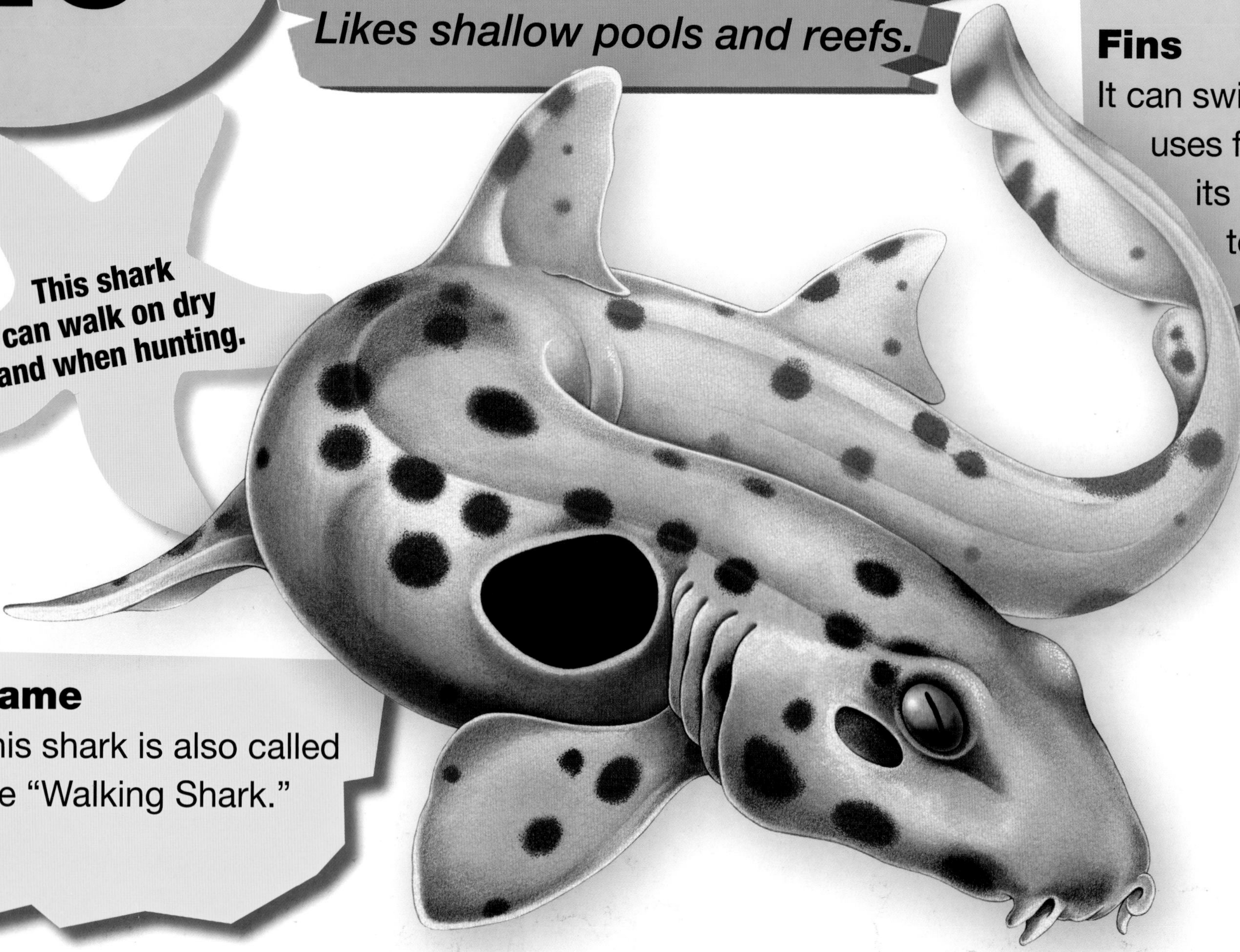

Fins
It can swim but also uses fins on its belly to "walk."

Name
This shark is also called the "Walking Shark."

Frilled Shark

Ff

Lives in very deep waters.

Mouth
It can swallow food larger than itself.

Gills
Gills help fish breathe. This shark's 6 rows of gills look like frills.

This shark has 300 teeth.

Gg

Great White Shark

Found in all oceans.

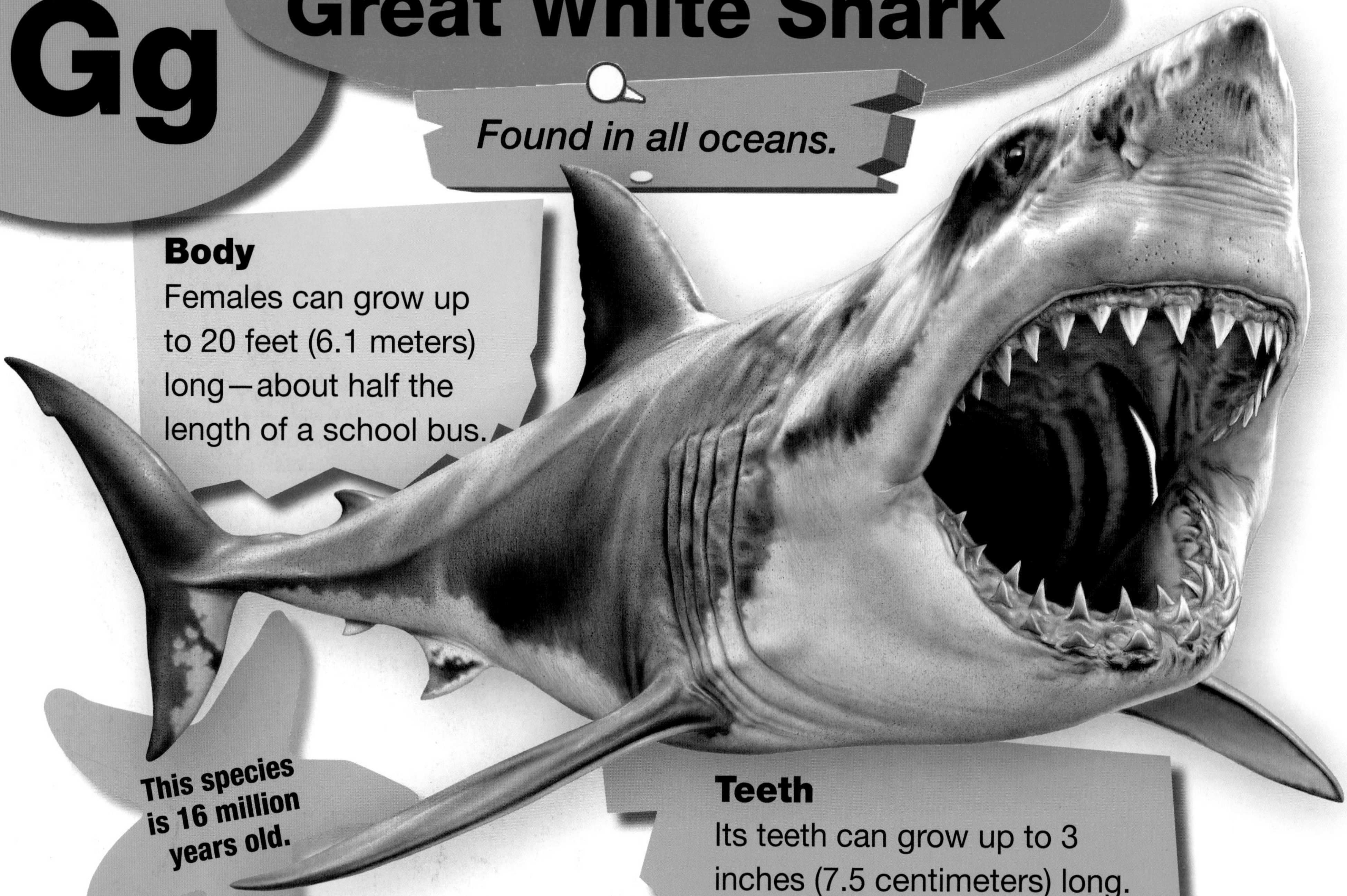

Body

Females can grow up to 20 feet (6.1 meters) long—about half the length of a school bus.

This species is 16 million years old.

Teeth

Its teeth can grow up to 3 inches (7.5 centimeters) long.

Hammerhead Shark

Hh

Lives in warm, coastal waters.

Head
Its long and flat head is shaped like a hammer.

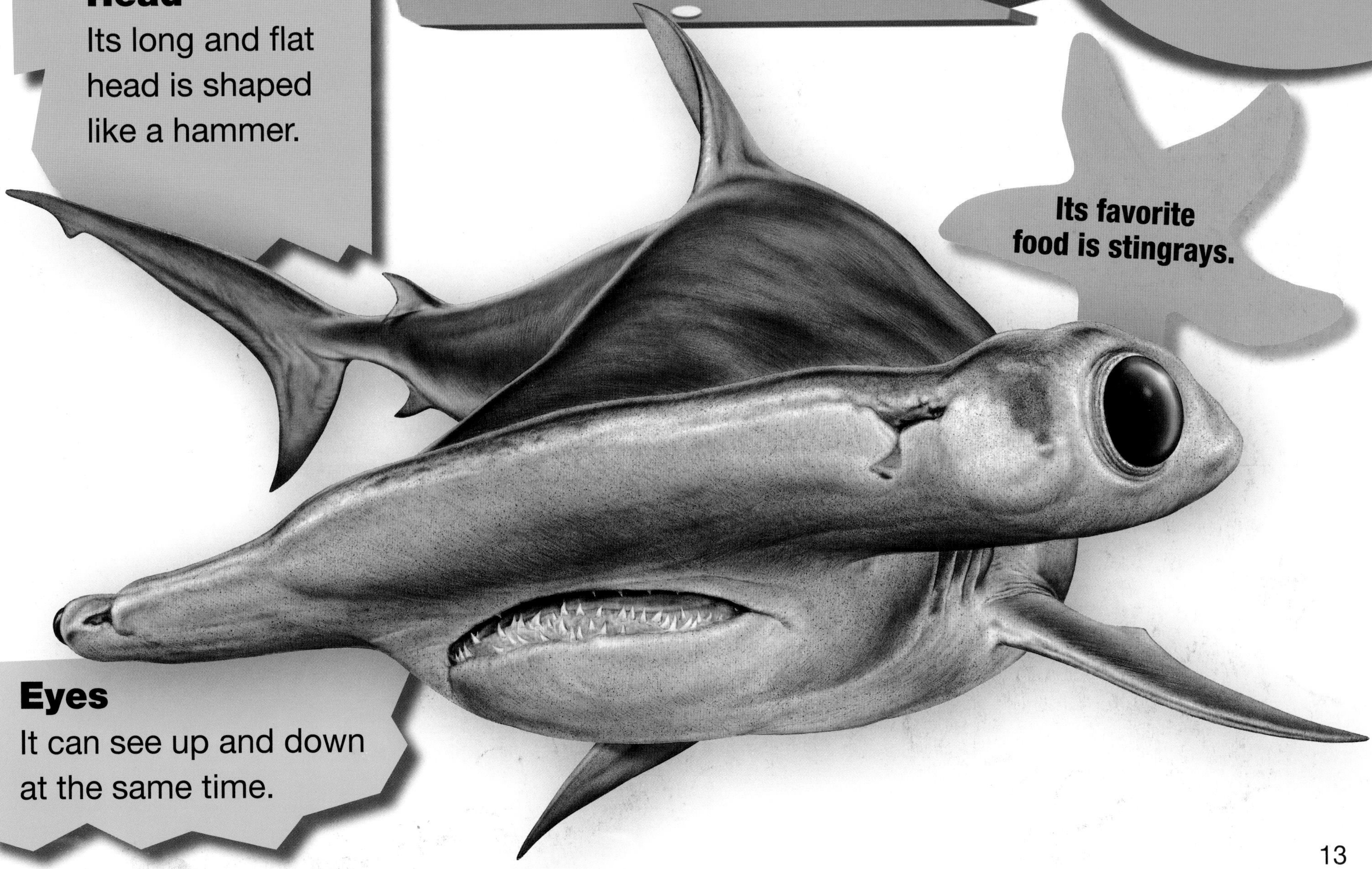

Its favorite food is stingrays.

Eyes
It can see up and down at the same time.

Ii Indonesian Speckled Carpet shark

Hunts at night.

Barbels
It has whiskers (barbels) to help it find food, even in muddy water.

It grows up to 18 inches (46 centimeters) in length.

Skin
Its skin pattern looks like a carpet.

Japanese Sawshark

Jj

Lives in muddy seabeds.

It eats small creatures buried in the mud.

Saw

Its saw-like nose has 25 to 45 teeth on each side.

Fins

Its fins are protected by rough scales called “denticles.”

Kk Kitefin Shark

Powerful deep-sea hunter.

Mouth
It will take bites out of bigger sharks and even whales.

This shark has 3 to 16 pups at a time.

Deep Water
It lives in water up to 3,280 feet (1,000 meters) deep.

Lemon Shark

Ll

Lives in or near mangroves.

Camouflage
Its color helps it hide when hunting over sandy seabeds.

It grows up to 11 feet (3.4 meters) in length.

Smart
This shark likes living with other sharks. They learn from one another.

Mm Megamouth Shark

Fewer than 100 ever seen.

This shark was discovered in 1976.

Mouth
This shark swims with its mouth open to eat up tiny water creatures.

Glowing
Parts of its mouth can glow in the dark to attract food.

Nurse Shark

Nn

Slow-moving reef shark.

Mouth
This shark sucks food in and uses its strong jaws to crush shellfish.

Slurping
When feeding, it makes a “slurping” noise that no other shark makes.

It grows up to 10 feet (3 meters) in length.

Oo Oceanic Whitetip Shark

Found in deep, open waters.

Body
This shark is rare because it's hunted for its fins, skin, and meat.

This shark eats anything, including whale waste.

Mouth
Its strong jaws are dangerous. It's known for attacks on people.

Port Jackson Shark

Pp

Found near Port Jackson, Australia.

Large Liver
Shark livers contain oil. Oil is lighter than water. This helps a shark float.

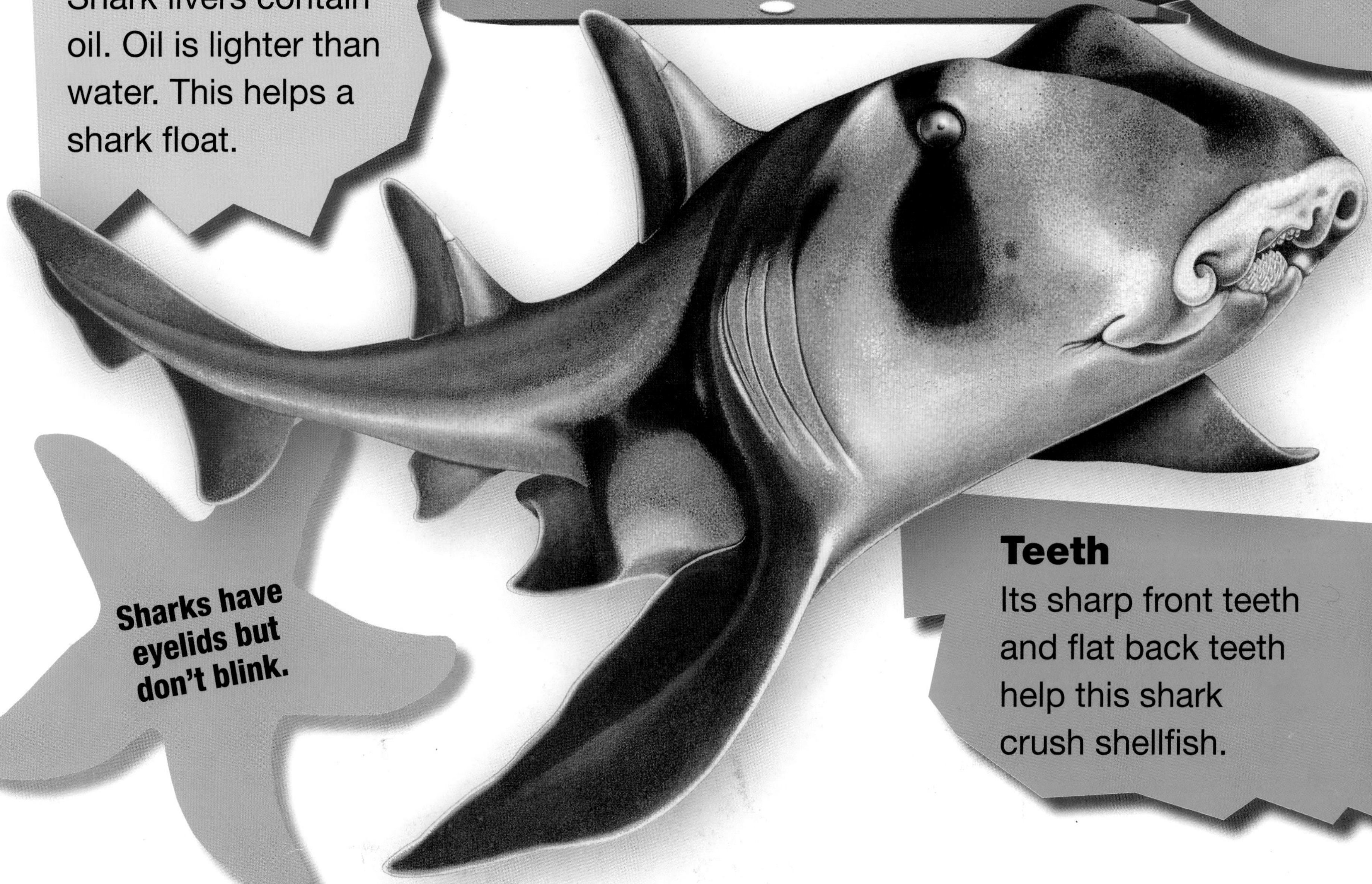

Sharks have eyelids but don't blink.

Teeth
Its sharp front teeth and flat back teeth help this shark crush shellfish.

Qq Quagga Catshark

Rare deep-sea hunter.

Zebra
These stripes give it its name. A quagga is a type of zebra.

See-Through Lids
Eyelids protect its eyes from dust and keep the eyes from drying out.

Fewer than 10 have ever been seen.

Roughshark

Rr

Deep-water shark.

Feeding
It eats worms, shellfish, and mollusks.

Gills
To breathe, sharks need to keep moving to push water through their gills.

The scales on this shark are rough, like teeth.

Ss Sand Tiger Shark

Found near sandy shores.

It is not related to a tiger shark.

Length
This shark is over 3 feet (1 meter) long when it is born.

Mouth
This shark gulps air into its stomach to help it float while hunting.

Tiger Shark

Tt

Likes warm waters around the world.

This shark's pups have tiger stripes.

Feeding
It is a dangerous shark and eats almost anything, from sick whales to trash.

Stomach
Horses, flying foxes, and cats have been found in the bellies of tiger sharks.

Uu Unusual Sharks

Are weird and wonderful.

Goblin Shark (shown below)
It has a very long nose that looks like the blade of a sword.

Thresher Shark
It's unusual because it cracks its massive tail, like a whip, to stun its food.

Basking and whale sharks are quite unusual, too.

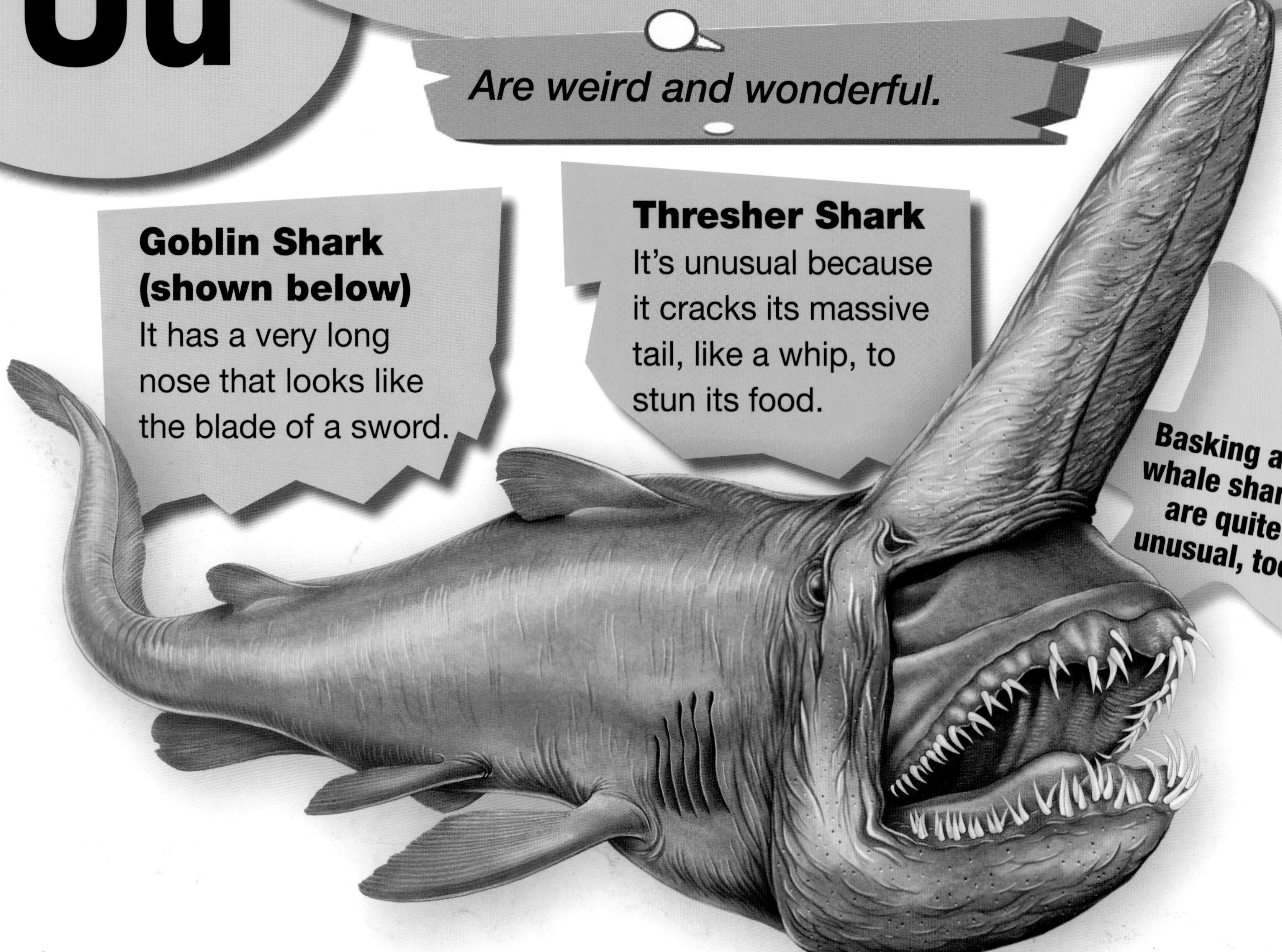

Velvet Belly Lanternshark

Vv

Likes cool, deep waters.

Camouflage
Its belly glows, making this shark hard to see from the ocean floor.

It grows up to 24 inches (61 centimeters) in length.

Belly
Light organs along the belly make this shark glow in the dark.

Ww Wobbegong

Spends its time on the seabed.

It's a type of carpet shark.

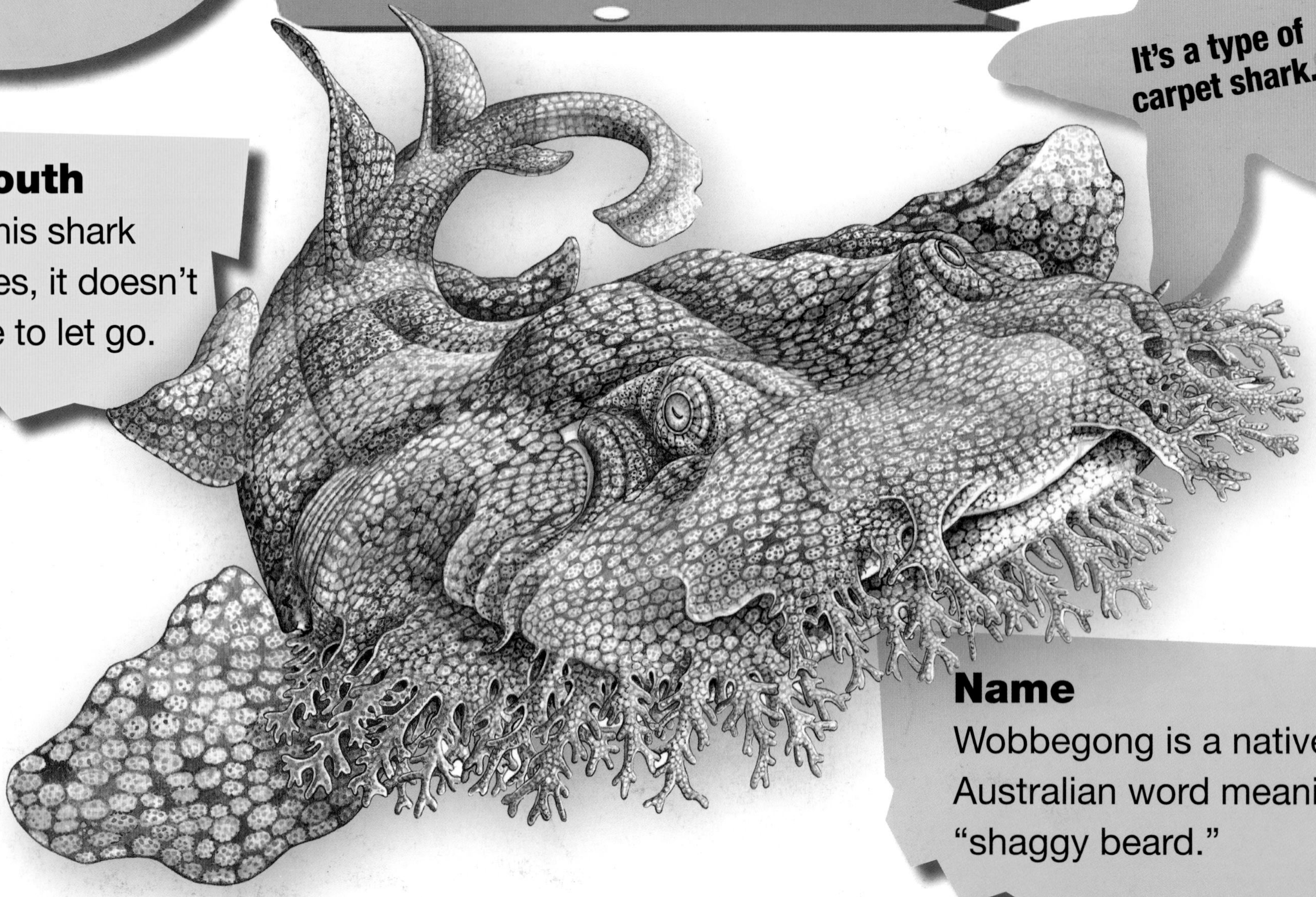

Mouth
If this shark bites, it doesn't like to let go.

Name
Wobbegong is a native Australian word meaning "shaggy beard."

Xenacanthus

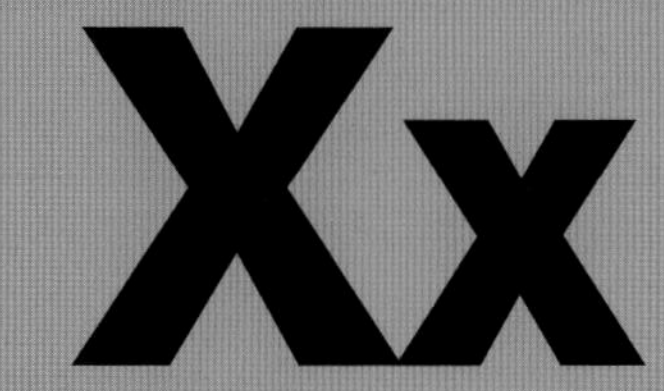

River-loving prehistoric shark.

Spine
Its bony spine scared attackers and may have held poison.

It died out 208 million years ago.

Bones
A shark's skeleton is not made of hard bones. Usually, only teeth survive as fossils.

Yy Yellow-Spotted Catshark

In seas around Southern Africa.

Eyes
It's named for its long, cat-like eyes.

This shark can live for 75 years.

Eggs
Catsharks lay eggs, known as mermaid's purses, on the seafloor.

Zebra Shark

Zz

Bottom-living carpet shark.

Stripes
Its pups have zebra stripes. The adults have spots.

A group of sharks is called a shiver.

Tail
Its long tail helps it swim fast and turn suddenly.

Aa
Angel Shark

Bb
Bull Shark

Cc
Caribbean Reef Shark

Dd
Dogfish Shark

Ee
Epaulette Shark

Ff
Frilled Shark

Gg
Great White Shark

Hh
Hammerhead Shark

Ii
Indonesian Speckled Carpet Shark

Jj
Japanese Sawshark

Kk
Kitefin Shark

Ll
Lemon Shark

Mm
Megamouth Shark

Nn
Nurse Shark

Oo
Oceanic Whitetip Shark

Pp
Port Jackson Shark

Qq
Quagga Catshark

Rr
Roughshark

Ss
Sand Tiger Shark

Tt
Tiger Shark

Uu
Unusual Sharks

Vv
Velvet Belly Lanternshark

Ww
Wobbegong

Xx
Xenacanthus

Yy
Yellow-Spotted Catshark

Zz
Zebra Shark